W9-AET-862

Get Well Soon!

I Have
Strep Throat

Gillian Gosman

PowerKiDS
press
New York

Published in 2013 by The Rosen Publishing Group, Inc.
29 East 21st Street, New York, NY 10010

First Edition

Editor: Jennifer Way
Book Design: Greg Tucker
Layout Design: Kate Laczynski

Photo Credits: Cover © www.iStockphoto.com/ Joshua Hodge Photography; pp 4–5 Paul Bradbury/OJO Images/ Getty Images; p. 6 © www.iStockphoto.com/Nina Shannon; p. 7 Tetra Images/Getty Images; p. 8 Dr. Fred Hossler/ Visuals Unlimited/Getty Images; p. 9 (top) Dorling Kindersley/the Agency Collection/Getty Images; p. 9 (bottom) Hemera/Thinkstock; p. 10 Scott Camazine/Photo Researchers/Getty Images; p. 11 Doctor Stock/Science Faction/ Getty Images; p. 12 © www.iStockphoto.com/Ana Abejon; pp. 13, 22 Shutterstock.com; p. 14 Goodshoot/Thinkstock; p. 15 (top) Brand X Pictures/Jupiterimages/Thinkstock; p. 15 (bottom) iStockphoto/Thinkstock; pp. 16–17 Frank Siteman/Science Faction/Getty Images; p. 18 © www.iStockphoto.com/kate_sept2004; p. 19 Creatas/Getty Images/ Thinkstock; p. 20 Stockbyte/George Doyle/Thinkstock; p. 21 © www.iStockphoto.com/Josh Rinehults.

Library of Congress Cataloging-in-Publication Data

Gosman, Gillian.
 I have strep throat / by Gillian Gosman. — 1st ed.
     p. cm. — (Get well soon!)
 Includes index.
 ISBN 978-1-4488-7412-5 (library binding)
 1. Streptococcal infections—Juvenile literature. 2. Throat—Diseases—Juvenile literature. I. Title.
 RC116.S84G67 2013
 616.9'298—dc23
                                        2011050677

Manufactured in the United States of America

CPSIA Compliance Information: Batch #SW12PK: For Further Information contact Rosen Publishing, New York, New York at 1-800-237-9932

Contents

I Have Strep Throat

You come home from school feeling terrible. Your throat really hurts. Every time you try to swallow, it feels like someone is squeezing your throat. It feels like you are trying to swallow nails. Your throat feels dry, scratchy, bumpy, and raw. You have a case of strep throat.

Strep throat feels terrible. Once you visit the doctor and begin taking medicine, though, you will start to get better. This book will tell you what happens when you get strep throat, how to treat it, and how to prevent it.

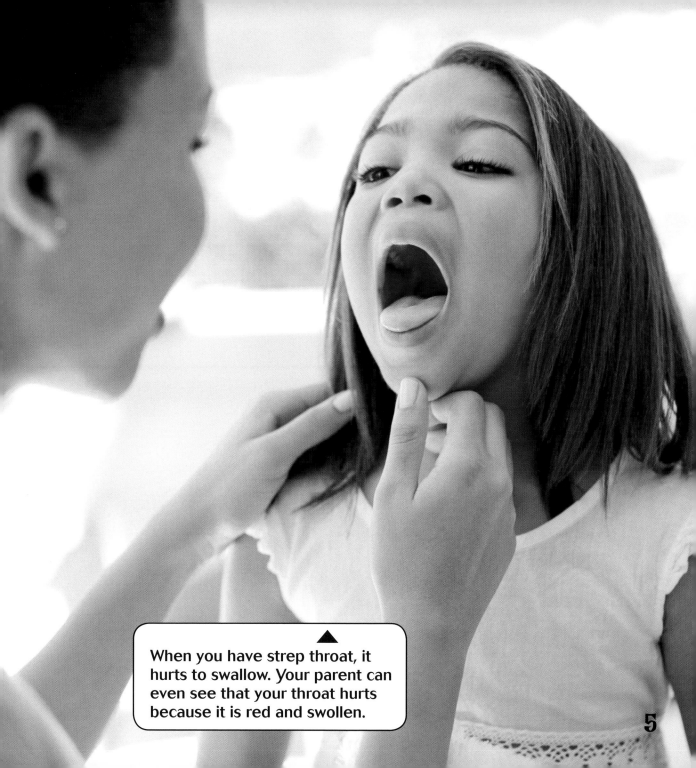

When you have strep throat, it hurts to swallow. Your parent can even see that your throat hurts because it is red and swollen.

What Is Strep Throat?

Bacteria cause strep throat. This throat **infection** feels much worse than other sore throats. With medicine given to you by a doctor and plenty of rest, though, most people beat strep throat in just a few days.

The bacteria that cause strep throat can cause other illnesses, though. Strep throat can lead to ear infections and kidney problems. It can also cause less common but

When you have strep throat, you will usually have a fever.

6

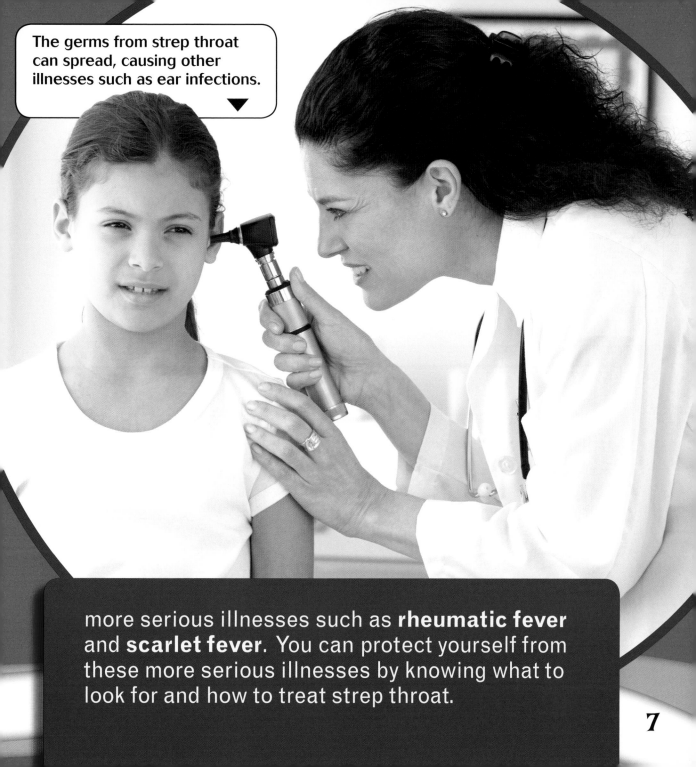

The germs from strep throat can spread, causing other illnesses such as ear infections. ▼

more serious illnesses such as **rheumatic fever** and **scarlet fever**. You can protect yourself from these more serious illnesses by knowing what to look for and how to treat strep throat.

What Causes Strep Throat?

Here are *Streptococcus pyogenes* bacteria, which cause strep throat. Individual round bacteria often join together in chainlike formations.

▼

"Strep throat" is the shortened name for the bacteria that cause this sickness. This bacteria is called *Streptococcus pyogenes*. "Streptococcus" comes from Greek words meaning "twisted berry." This is a good name for the bacteria because they look like tangled strings of berries. Bacteria are tiny living things, no bigger than **cells**. You can see them

The pain from a case of strep throat usually comes on suddenly and severely. ▶

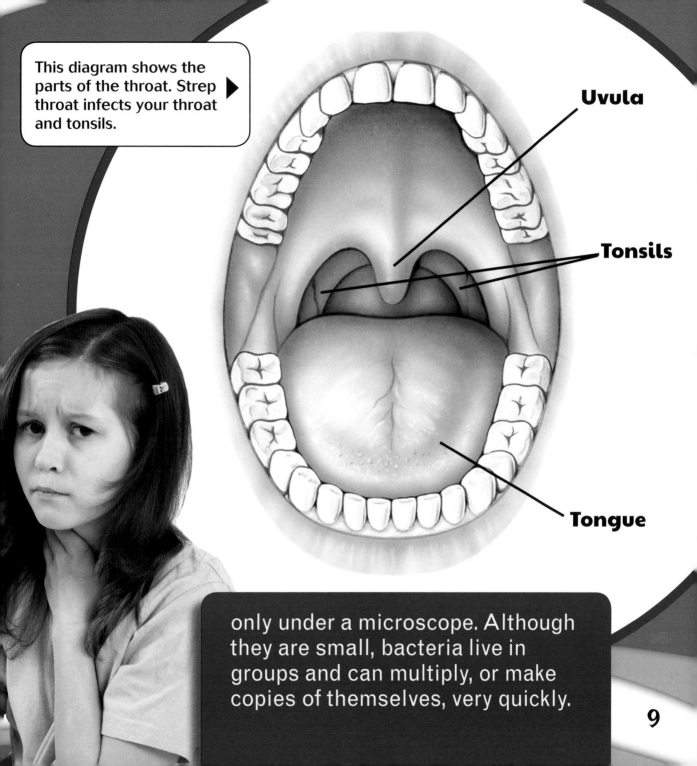

This diagram shows the parts of the throat. Strep throat infects your throat and tonsils. ▶

Uvula

Tonsils

Tongue

only under a microscope. Although they are small, bacteria live in groups and can multiply, or make copies of themselves, very quickly.

Signs and Symptoms

When you have strep throat, you have both **signs** and **symptoms**. Signs are the things a doctor can find out by examining a patient. Doctors note that patients with strep throat have swollen **glands** in their necks. They may also have a fever and may have white, bumpy patches inside their throats.

> Here you can see white patches on swollen tonsils. This is a sign of strep throat.

When you go to the doctor, you describe the symptoms of your illness, such as a sore throat.

The information a patient gives about how he is feeling is called his symptoms. Patients with strep throat often tell doctors that they do not feel like eating, and their throats hurt a lot.

11

What's Going On in My Body?

Bacteria can live on their own. However, if they find a host, such as the cells in your throat, they can quickly multiply and spread. When this happens, this is called an infection.

Your body's **immune system** works to fight an infection like strep throat. The immune system tries to make

When your immune system is fighting an illness, it often leaves you feeling tired. That is why it is important to rest while you are sick with strep throat.

the body a bad place for bacteria to live. For example, it will raise your body temperature. We experience the immune system's response as aches, pains, fever, and sleepiness.

▲

Fever is a sign that your body is fighting an infection. A cool washcloth on your forehead can help relieve the discomfort you feel.

How Did I Catch Strep Throat?

Illnesses like strep throat can spread quickly at schools because they are places where lots of people are together. ▼

Strep throat bacteria are very **contagious.** This means it is very easy to catch strep throat from other people. Bacteria travel from one person to another in tiny drops of mucus, the liquid in your nose and mouth. When a sick person coughs, sneezes, or wipes her nose, mucus is let out into the air.

Sneezing into a tissue, and then throwing the tissue away and washing your hands helps stop the spread of germs. ▶

Unwashed hands can carry lots of different germs. Shaking hands and then touching your nose or mouth is one way you can pick up germs like strep throat bacteria.

Hopefully, that germy mucus lands in a tissue. If not, the germs could land on the sick person's hands, on a table, doorknob, or some other hard surface. From there, another person can pick up the germs.

Going to the Doctor

Strep throat is easy to treat. Because the infection can lead to more serious problems, it is important to visit the doctor if you think you might have strep throat. If you have a very painful sore throat that lasts longer than two days, a fever, and swollen lymph nodes, be sure to visit the doctor.

To find out whether a patient has strep throat, the doctor will rub a cotton swab across the back of the patient's throat. The cotton will be sent to a lab and tested for the bacteria that cause strep throat.

To do a strep test, the doctor will swab the back of your throat. This test can tell her you have strep throat in just a few minutes. ▶

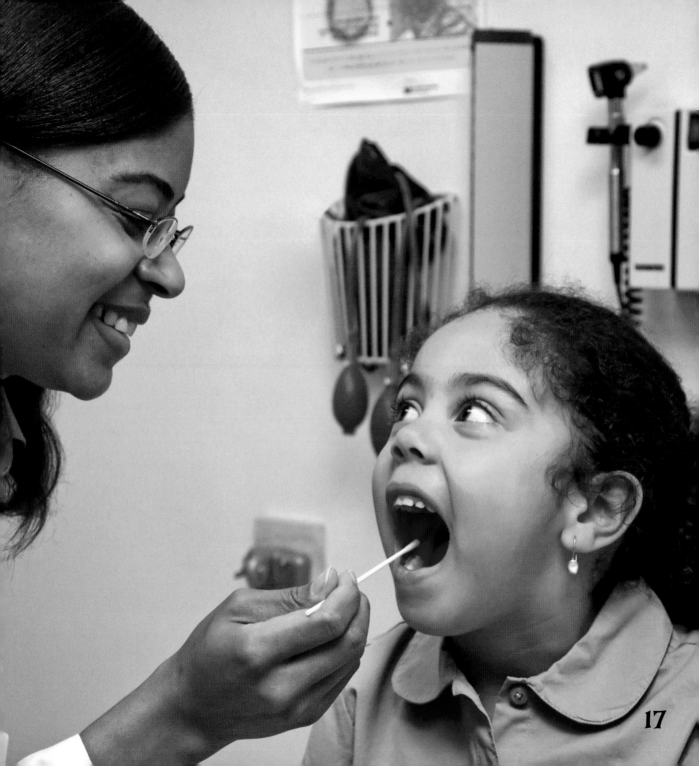

How Strep Throat Is Treated

A doctor will **prescribe** medicine called antibiotics for strep throat. The antibiotics are usually taken for 10 days. The signs and symptoms of strep throat start to go away after a day or two of taking the medicine. You need to finish the medicine to make sure all of the strep bacteria are killed, though.

◄ Eating warm soup can soothe your throat pain. It may hurt to swallow, but it is important to eat!

When you have strep throat, you should drink plenty of liquids. This will help your fever and make sure your body has the water it needs.

You should treat your throat well when you have strep throat. Drinking warm drinks and eating ice pops may soothe your throat pain. You can also take over-the-counter pain relievers for your fever and sore throat.

How to Prevent Strep Throat

Strep throat is easily passed from person to person. In order to stay healthy, avoid people who are sick with strep throat. If you have strep throat, do not go to school until you have been on antibiotics for two or more days. After that point, you will no longer be contagious. Washing

Washing dishes and utensils separately in hot, soapy water is a good way to keep from spreading strep throat germs to other people in your home.

Warm, soapy water is the best way to clean your hands. Hand sanitizers are good for cleaning your hands when you are on the go, though.

your hands and cleaning common surfaces are other good ways to keep germs from spreading. Patients who get strep throat again and again may be told to get an operation in which the **tonsils** are removed. This operation has been shown to prevent frequent throat infections.

The Road to Recovery

Just a day or two after starting antibiotics for strep throat, you will start feeling better. You should be sure to rest, drink plenty of water, and begin to eat more. After you are better, you should replace your toothbrush so that you do not give yourself strep throat germs again.

Taking antibiotics will make you start to feel better quickly. You will still be contagious, so it is best if you stay home for a few days.

Now you know more about staying healthy and avoiding strep throat. You also know what to do if you catch it.

Glossary

bacteria (bak-TIR-ee-uh) Tiny living things that cannot be seen with the eye alone. Some bacteria cause illness or rotting, but others are helpful.

cells (SELZ) The basic units of living things.

contagious (kun-TAY-jus) Able to be passed on.

glands (GLANDZ) Organs or parts of the body that produce elements to help with bodily functions.

immune system (ih-MYOON SIS-tem) The system that keeps the body safe from sicknesses.

infection (in-FEK-shun) A sickness caused by germs.

prescribe (prih-SKRYB) To order a certain kind of medicine.

rheumatic fever (roo-MA-tik FEE-ver) An illness that causes pain and high fever.

scarlet fever (SKAR-let FEE-ver) An illness that is marked by a fever and breaking out into red spots.

signs (SYNZ) Things that show that one might have an illness.

symptoms (SIMP-tumz) Information patients give doctors about illnesses based on what they are feeling.

tonsils (TONT-sulz) Parts of the body that lie on either side of the throat.

Index

Websites

Due to the changing nature of Internet links, PowerKids Press has developed an online list of websites related to the subject of this book. This site is updated regularly. Please use this link to access the list: www.powerkidslinks.com/gws/strep/